MAJOR
A SOLDIER DOG

TREVOR JONES
ILLUSTRATED BY
MING HAI

PUBLISHED IN ASSOCIATION WITH
HISTORY NEBRASKA

SIX FOOT PRESS

HOUSTON • LOS ANGELES

When I was little, my best friend was Sid. He smelled like soap, dirt, and syrup, and we played all day in the snow.
I loved to sleep close to him at night, where I heard branches on the roof and the snores of his parents.

One day, things changed. I could smell that Sid and my family were excited and a little scared, so I licked them. I did not know how to feel, so I barked a lot.

Soon after that, we got in the car. I licked tears from Sid's face while we drove. We arrived at a new place with loud thumping noises that hurt my ears. Two men grabbed me and tried to push me into a dirty box. I was scared, so I bit them.

Sid crawled in the box and called me, but he was crying and would not look at me. I got in the box to comfort him, but a hand pulled him out and the door slammed shut with a bang. I was trapped!

I traveled for a long time and arrived at a place with many people and even more smells. I was poked and marked and I did not enjoy that.
There were many other dogs of all sizes, and more were arriving all the time. I missed Sid, but at least I was not alone.

I made friends with other dogs, like Taffy and Poochie and Kimmel. They had all come from far away. We did not get to see each other every day, but we tried to let each other know we were fine. It was always loud with so many dogs talking at once, so sometimes it was hard to sleep.

Soon, I met a man named Zeke. He smelled like bacon and wool, and he needed my help climbing, running, and finding things. I was not always sure what he wanted me to do, but I wanted to make Zeke happy, so I did my best.

Taffy just wanted to chase sticks, cats, and people. She kept running away but they always caught her.

There were so many dogs,
and we all learned
different things.

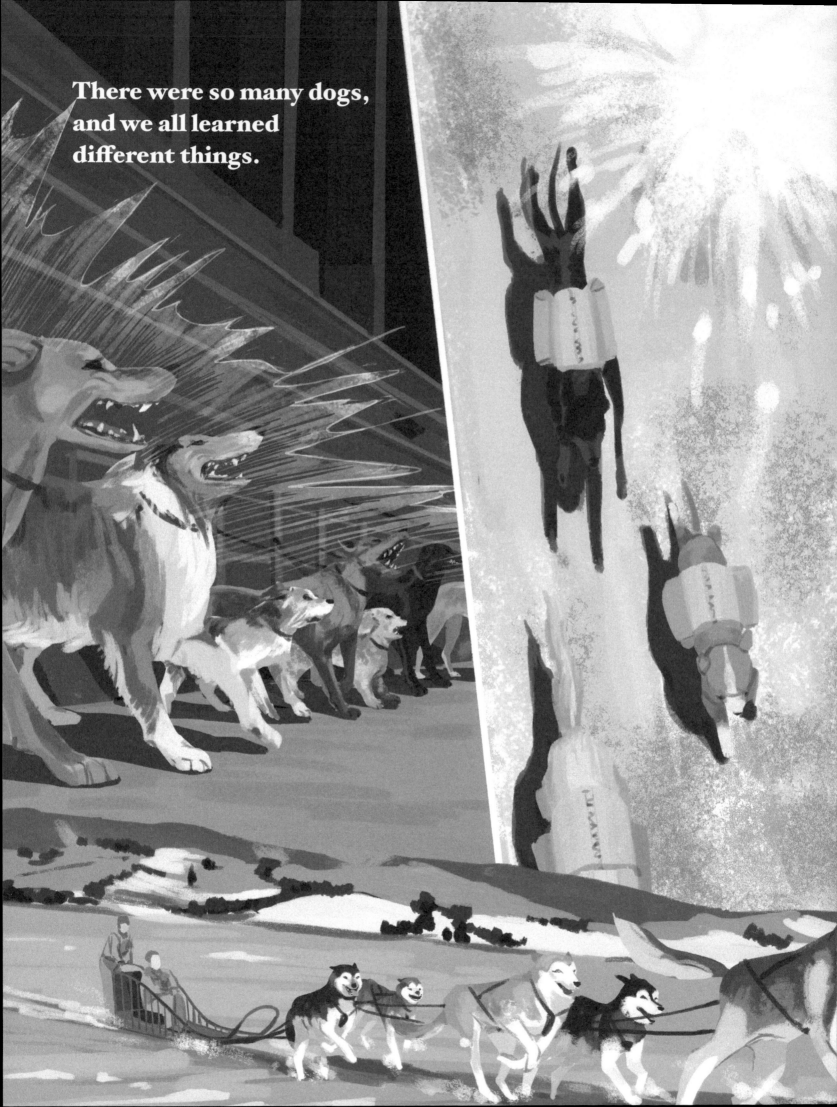

After
a while, they
threw a party for us.
I got some special treats and
Zeke got a piece of paper that I tried to eat.
They shipped us off again on a train that smelled like
oil and onions.
I was with friends and there were new people who
wanted to pet me, but that was not allowed.
Only Zeke could touch me.

The trip was scary. The water was much bigger than any water I had seen at home. It smelled like fish, but I could not find any! The way the boat moved made my stomach feel weird.

Days of playing seemed far away and the smells of Sid, my family, and my home faded.
There were booming sounds and smells of burning tires, but I wanted to help Zeke and he needed me. We were always tired and dirty and Zeke smelled scared much of the time.
Every day, we went for long walks where I paid attention to strange sounds and smells.

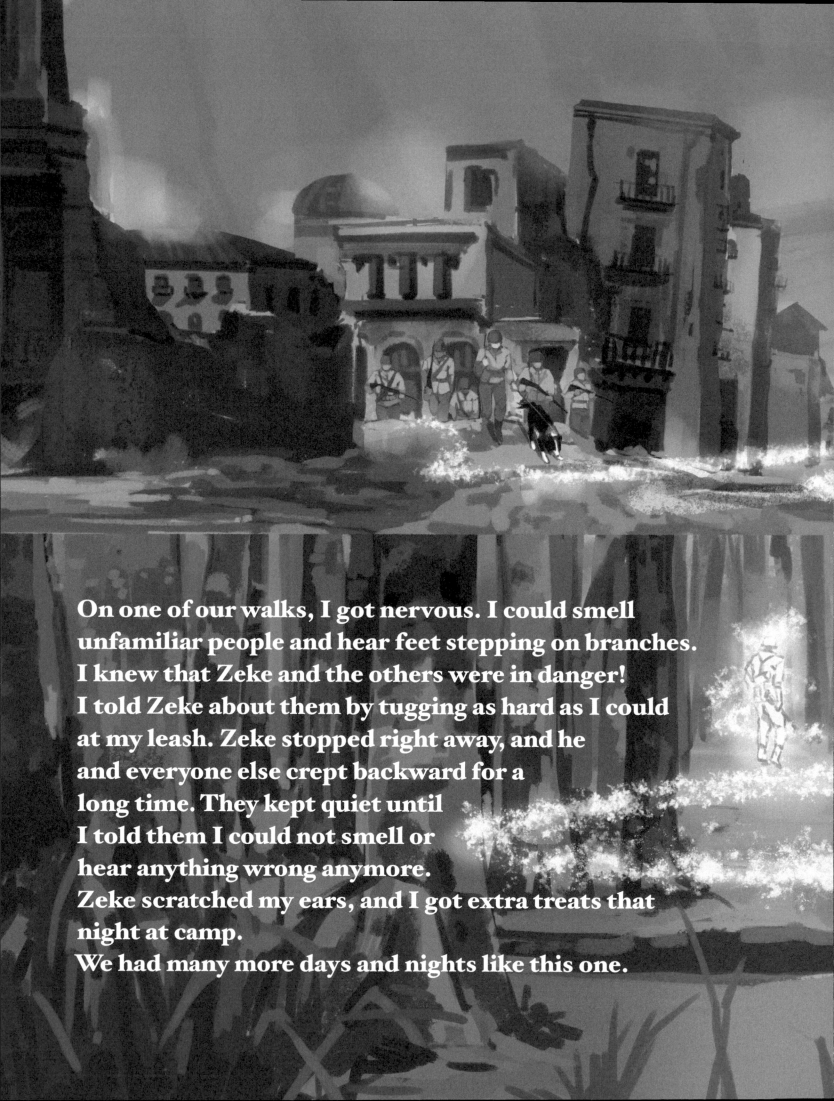

On one of our walks, I got nervous. I could smell unfamiliar people and hear feet stepping on branches. I knew that Zeke and the others were in danger! I told Zeke about them by tugging as hard as I could at my leash. Zeke stopped right away, and he and everyone else crept backward for a long time. They kept quiet until I told them I could not smell or hear anything wrong anymore. Zeke scratched my ears, and I got extra treats that night at camp.
We had many more days and nights like this one.

Finally, after what seemed like a long time, the men in the camp gathered one morning. Their leader said words in a happy voice and everyone started cheering! I did not know what happened, but I knew it was good news. I started barking and they did not even tell me to be quiet.

Soon we got back on a large boat and went back across the water, but this time everyone smelled happy and laughed a lot. I got all the treats I wanted.

Once we got off the boat, I got on a train that smelled like chocolate, but Zeke would not give me any. When it stopped, we had returned to where I met Zeke for the first time. The smells of my friends had faded so much I could barely make them out. Even worse, Zeke left, and I worried about being lonely.

A new person, Carol, started taking care of me and other
dogs. She had a gentle voice and smiling eyes. She asked me
to do different things. Instead of barking at people I did not
know, I had to sit still. She let everyone pet me instead of only
Zeke. I liked that part. It was not hard to learn, but it was
different from being with Zeke. When the other dogs and I did
something Carol liked, she gave us treats.

One day, Carol gave me a hug and a smile and put me into a crate smelling like fresh pine. I was sad to leave, but there was nothing to do but sleep and smell the world going by. When the train stopped, the crate opened and someone was there! He was bigger so I was not sure at first, but as soon as I smelled and licked him, I knew it was my old friend Sid!

Now I play with other dogs, and I am gentle with the small ones. Sometimes the old smells come back to me, and I remember my trip across the water and back. I even got my picture in the paper and people thank me for what I did. I am happy that I helped Zeke and his friends, but I am even happier to curl up with Sid, safe and sound.

Major and Sid, 1942.

Carol Roever (later Simmons) in
her dog training gear, 1944-45.

Everything in *Major: A Soldier Dog* is based in fact. After the United States entered World
War II, a group of people led by famed dog breeder Alene Erlanger (look for her when
Major graduates training school) started a group called Dogs for Defense. The military
needed war dogs to patrol factories, serve as messengers, scout, and detect mines, but
they did not have any on hand. Dogs for Defense called on patriotic Americans to enlist
their pets in the Army. Thousands of people sent their pets away to help the war effort,
with no idea if they would ever see them again.

In Wahpeton, North Dakota, five-year-old Sid Moore's family sent Major, the family
dog, off to war. Climbing inside the shipping crate to lure Major inside was Sid's worst
childhood memory. Sid can still hear the noise the crate made when it slammed shut and
Major left for Nebraska.

Richard "Zeke" Zika at the gates of the War Dog Training Center at Fort Robinson, 1943.

There were several dog training centers, but the most important was Fort Robinson, Nebraska, with over 14,000 dogs. Major trained there, along with a skinny young man from Detroit named Richard "Zeke" Zika. Thousands of soldiers and dogs worked together, including Taffy, Poochie, and Kimmel, although Taffy did run away a lot! The dogs fought all over the world—in the South Pacific, Europe, and everywhere in between. We do not know exactly where Major went, but we have a lot of information about dogs in Italy, so we sent Major and Zeke there (even though the real Zeke actually went to India). Dogs saved many American soldiers' lives by alerting them to ambushes, and the war dog training program became the model for training military dogs today.

Major and Sid, 1943.

When the war was over, the government worked hard to send dogs back to their owners. First, the dogs went to Fort Robinson in Nebraska to learn how to be pets again. One of their trainers was Carol Roever Simmons, who worked with hundreds of dogs at the end of the war. Many women's stories are not in history books, and Carol does not appear in the official records of Fort Robinson. Even so, we have her own accounts of her experience and pictures of her working, so we know she was there.

Once the dogs were ready to leave the military, the Army sent them back home. They did this for free and also sent discharge papers—just as they did with human soldiers. The dogs were veterans, and Major was welcomed back at Sid's house as a hero.

If you want to see real pictures of World War II dogs or visit the place where Major became a soldier dog, visit History Nebraska's website at www.history.nebraska.gov.